BRAZIL

TRAVEL GUIDE 2023

The Complete Pocket Guide to Discover Brazil's Best, Art & Culture, Food, Dance, Wildlife, and Off-the-Beaten-Path Destinations. Everything You Need for a Memorable Trip

SETH HICKSON

Copyright 2023, Seth Hickson.

All rights reserved.

No part of this publication may be reproduced, distributed, or transmitted in any form or by any means, including photocopying, recording, or other electronic or mechanical methods, without the prior written permission of the publisher, except in the case of brief quotations embodied in critical reviews and certain other noncommercial uses permitted by copyright law.

TABLE OF CONTENTS

INTRODUCTION
- About the Country
- Landscapes
- Samba and Carnival
- Cultural Diversity

PLANNING YOUR TRIP TO BRAZIL
- When to Visit
- Visa and Entry Requirements
- Travel Insurance
- Health Precautions
- Packing Essentials
- Language and Communication

GETTING AROUND BRAZIL
- Transportation
- Safety Tips for Travelers

TOP DESTINATIONS IN BRAZIL
- Rio de Janeiro
- São Paulo
- Salvador

- Manaus
- Florianópolis
- Brasília

OFF-THE-BEATEN-PATH DESTINATIONS IN BRAZIL
- Paraty
- Lençóis Maranhenses National Park
- Bonito
- Jericoacoara
- Chapada Diamantina
- Ouro Preto

BRAZILIAN CUISINE
- Must-Try Brazilian Dishes
- Regional Specialties
- Popular Restaurants and Food Markets

CULTURAL EXPERIENCES
- Carnival in Brazil
- Capoeira and Brazilian Martial Arts
- Samba and Forró Dance
- Indigenous Culture and Communities
- Religious Festivals and Traditions

OUTDOOR ACTIVITIES & ADVENTURE
- Beach Activities and Water Sports
- Hiking in National Parks
- Wildlife Watching and Eco-Tours
- Surfing and Kitesurfing Spots
- Scuba Diving and Snorkeling

BRAZIL'S RICH WILDLIFE
- The Amazon Rainforest and its wildlife
- Pantanal Wetlands
- Atlantic Forest Biodiversity
- Birdwatching Hotspots

TRAVELING WITH SPECIAL INTERESTS
- Family-friendly Activities
- LGBTQ+ Travelers' Guide
- Solo Travel Tips
- Adventure Enthusiast's Itinerary

PRACTICAL TIPS FOR TRAVELERS
- Currency and Money Matters
- Safety and Security

- Local Etiquette and Customs
- Internet and Connectivity
- Language and Basic Phrases

SUSTAINABLE TRAVEL AND ECOTOURISM
- Supporting Local Communities
- Reducing Environmental Impact
- Eco-friendly Accommodation
- Respectful Interactions with Wildlife

INTRODUCTION

Welcome to Brazil, the biggest nation in South America and the fifth-largest in the world by both land and population. Known for its lively culture, gorgeous landscapes, and vast wildlife, Brazil delivers a captivating experience to everyone who comes. From the busy city of Rio de Janeiro and São Paulo to the Amazon jungle and the magnificent beaches along the Atlantic coast, Brazil is a place of contrasts, rich history, and distinct cultures.

About the Country

Brazil, formally known as the Federative Republic of Brazil, has a large territory of about 8.5 million square kilometers and is home to around 212 million people (as of my latest knowledge update in September 2021). The republic shares borders with eleven other South American countries, including Argentina, Uruguay, Paraguay, Bolivia, Peru, Colombia, Venezuela, Guyana, Suriname, and French Guiana. The official language is Portuguese, making Brazil the sole Portuguese-speaking nation in South America.

Brazil's history stretches back to the indigenous peoples who inhabited the area for thousands of years before the advent of European explorers. In 1500, the Portuguese explorer Pedro Álvares Cabral claimed the land for Portugal, leading to centuries of colonization and the foundation of a Portuguese monarchy in the early 19th century. Brazil achieved its independence in 1822 and has since grown into a democratic country with a diversified cultural legacy.

Landscapes

Encompassing roughly half of South America's area, Brazil features some of the most breathtaking natural marvels on the globe. The Amazon Rainforest, commonly referred to as the "lungs of the Earth," is a biodiverse wonderland overflowing with unique plants and wildlife. Marvel at the sight of uncommon animals, such as jaguars, macaws, and pink dolphins, as you go deep into the heart of the forest.

Along Brazil's 7,491 kilometers (4,655 miles) of coastline, you'll discover a treasure trove of gorgeous beaches. Sunbathe on the world-famous Copacabana and Ipanema beaches in Rio de Janeiro or explore the calm shores of Fernando de Noronha, an island featuring crystal-clear seas and diverse marine life, making it a paradise for snorkelers and scuba divers.

Samba and Carnival

Brazil is linked with music and dancing, and nothing symbolizes its soul more than samba. This addictive Afro-Brazilian beat has deep roots in the country's culture and is celebrated throughout the year in boisterous gatherings and street festivals. Yet, it is during Carnival when the genuine spirit of samba comes to life. Join the celebrations in

Rio de Janeiro, Salvador, or São Paulo, where millions of revelers dance to the beat of the drums, sporting extravagant costumes and contagious grins.

Cultural Diversity

Brazil's cultural richness is a monument to its history of indigenous, European, African, and Asian influences. The indigenous peoples, who were the earliest residents of the territory, have left their stamp on the country's art, food, and customs. Despite the problems they encounter, indigenous tribes continue to retain their historic knowledge and traditional customs.

The entrance of Portuguese explorers in the 16th century introduced European influences that affected Brazil's language (Portuguese), religion (predominantly Catholic), and architecture. The combination of European conventions with native traditions gave birth to a distinct Brazilian identity that continues strong today.

During the colonial period, the slave trade brought millions of Africans to Brazil, enhancing the country's culture with their music, dancing, and culinary contributions. Afro-Brazilian traditions, such as capoeira and Candomblé, have become fundamental components of the country's cultural fabric.

In more recent times, Brazil has experienced waves of immigration from numerous corners of the globe, including Italy, Germany, Japan, and the Middle East. These immigrant populations have brought extra complexity and variety to Brazilian culture.

The arts and music have a vital part in Brazilian culture. From the explosive rhythms of samba and bossa nova to the expressive motions of capoeira, music, and dance are profoundly interwoven in the lives of Brazilians. Additionally, Brazilian literature, film, and visual arts have earned worldwide attention, demonstrating the country's skill and originality.

As you flip through the pages of this Travel Guide, you'll uncover the spirit of this enchanting country. Immerse yourself in Brazil's cultural opulence, embrace the warmth of its people, and let its natural beauty leave you awe-inspired. Whether you want the rhythmic pulses of samba, the beautiful vistas of the Amazon, or the thrill of adventure, Brazil promises to be an amazing experience that will grab your heart and soul, leaving you craving for more. Your trip awaits - let's go on this incredible voyage together.

PLANNING YOUR TRIP TO BRAZIL

When to Visit

Before going on your vacation to Brazil, it's crucial to examine the optimum time to visit, since the country's numerous regions encounter varying temperatures and weather patterns.

The peak tourist season in Brazil is between December and February when the weather is pleasant and sunny. This month is especially popular for visiting the coastal towns and beaches, like Rio de Janeiro and Salvador, where holidaymakers may experience the lively Carnival activities. However, bear in mind that this is also the busiest period for tourists, and rates for hotels and flights may be higher than during other months.

If you prefer warmer weather and fewer people, try visiting Brazil during the shoulder seasons: March to May and September to November. During these months, you may still enjoy comfortable weather and take advantage of more moderate pricing for lodgings and activities.

If you are interested in visiting the Amazon rainforest, it's better to travel during the dry season, which normally lasts from June to September. The dry season provides better access to the jungle, with fewer risks of severe rains and floods.

For those wanting to visit the Southern area, which includes cities like São Paulo and Porto Alegre, the winter months of June to August provide lower weather and an opportunity to see Brazilian culture in a new light.

Ultimately, the ideal time to visit Brazil depends on your choices and the exact places you choose to see. Regardless of the season, Brazil's beauty and warmth will leave you with wonderful memories.

Visa and Entry Requirements

Before traveling to Brazil, it's necessary to verify the visa and entrance requirements depending on your nationality. Brazil had adopted a visa exemption for citizens of numerous countries, including the United States, Canada, the United Kingdom, Australia, and most European Union member states, enabling them to remain in Brazil for up to 90 days for tourist reasons.

However, visa laws might vary, so it's vital to consult the official website of the Brazilian embassy or consulate in your country to verify the current requirements. If your nation needs a visa, ensure you apply well in advance of your trip dates.

During your admission into Brazil, you will be needed to provide a valid passport with at least six months of validity from your scheduled departure date. It's vital to have a physical or electronic copy of your return ticket, as well as evidence of adequate finances to support your stay in the nation.

Travel Insurance

Travel insurance is a vital aspect of trip preparation, and it's strongly suggested to get comprehensive coverage before flying to

Brazil. The correct travel insurance can give financial protection in case of unanticipated circumstances such as trip cancellations, medical crises, lost luggage, or aircraft delays.

When picking a travel insurance plan, verify that it contains appropriate medical coverage, as well as coverage for adventurous activities or excursions you want to partake in, such as trekking in the jungle or water sports along the coast. It's vital to read the policy completely and understand what is covered and any exclusions or limits.

In case of a medical emergency, Brazil offers both public and private healthcare services. While public healthcare is accessible, private hospitals often provide a superior degree of service. Having travel insurance will guarantee you access to the finest medical treatment and prevent any financial constraints.

Health Precautions

Before flying to Brazil, it's vital to see a travel medicine professional or your healthcare practitioner to acquire up-to-date information on required vaccines and health precautions.

As a tropical nation, Brazil is home to some illnesses that may not be prominent in other places. The most noteworthy problem is malaria, particularly in the Amazon jungle and rural regions. It's vital to take malaria prophylaxis if you want to visit these places.

Additionally, immunizations for yellow fever, hepatitis A and B, typhoid, and tetanus are generally advised for visitors visiting Brazil. Some passengers may additionally require confirmation of yellow fever vaccination to enter the country, particularly if they are traveling from countries where yellow fever is prevalent. Check the criteria on the World Health

Organization (WHO) website or visit your healthcare physician for tailored guidance.

To protect yourself against insect-borne diseases like dengue fever and Zika virus, apply insect repellent, wear long sleeves and trousers, and avoid outside activities during peak mosquito activity hours.

As with any overseas vacation, it's important to consume bottled or filtered water and avoid ingesting raw or undercooked meals to prevent stomach disorders.

Packing Essentials

Packing for Brazil needs consideration of the varying climate and numerous activities you may participate in during your vacation. Here are some basics to add to your packing list:

- **Lightweight Clothes:** Brazil's temperature may be hot and humid, so bring lightweight and breathable clothes. For coastal places, swimwear and beachwear are necessary.

- **Rain Gear:** If you intend to come during the rainy season, pack a small rain jacket or umbrella to remain dry.

- **Comfortable Shoes:** Bring comfortable walking shoes for city tours and, if needed, strong hiking boots for jungle trips.

- **Sun Protection:** Pack sunscreen with a high SPF, sunglasses, and a wide-brimmed hat to protect yourself from the harsh sun.

- **Insect Repellent:** Essential for defending against mosquito-borne infections.

- **Medications and First-Aid Kit:** Include any required medications, as well as a basic first-aid kit for minor accidents.

- **Electrical Adapters:** Brazil utilizes Type N electrical outlets, so ensure you have the right adapters for your gadgets.

- **Language Guidebook:** While English may be spoken in tourist places, owning a Portuguese phrasebook or language app might be beneficial for communicating.

- **Travel papers:** Keep copies of your passport, visa, travel insurance, and other critical papers in a different area from the originals.

Language and Communication

The official language of Brazil is Portuguese, and although English may be spoken in major tourist locations and hotels, learning some basic Portuguese phrases may be useful, particularly when dealing with residents in smaller towns or rural regions.

Consider downloading language apps or carrying a pocket-sized phrasebook to help you communicate and navigate through ordinary circumstances. The attempt to speak the local language is typically appreciated by Brazilians and might improve your vacation experience.

When it comes to communication, Brazil has a well-developed telecommunications network, with access to mobile phone services and the internet readily accessible in metropolitan areas. International roaming may be pricey, so consider acquiring a local SIM card or accessing Wi-Fi at hotels, cafés, and public areas.

Proper preparation is key for a successful vacation to Brazil. Understanding the ideal time to travel, visa restrictions, and health measures helps guarantee a comfortable voyage. Equipping yourself with travel insurance, basic gear, and some Portuguese language skills will improve your trip, enabling you to immerse yourself in Brazil's rich culture and different landscapes with confidence. From the busy metropolis to the virgin jungles, Brazil has something to offer every tourist, guaranteeing experiences that will last a lifetime.

GETTING AROUND BRAZIL

Brazil is a huge nation with varied landscapes and areas to visit. To make the most of your vacation, it's necessary to understand the transportation alternatives accessible for moving about Brazil. Whether you're traversing the busy metropolis or traveling into the secluded parts of the Amazon jungle, understanding the different types of transportation can help you have a smooth and pleasurable voyage.

Transportation

Air Travel

Air travel is the most effective and comfortable option to traverse big distances inside Brazil, particularly if you want to visit various parts of the nation. Brazil has an extensive network of airports, with major towns and important tourist locations well-connected by domestic flights.

The primary airline carriers in Brazil are LATAM Airlines, Gol Linhas Aéreas, and Azul Brazilian Airlines. These airlines run daily flights between major cities, making it easier to move from one location to another fast.

When buying domestic flights, it's important to plan to receive the cheapest pricing. Flight fares might vary based on the time of year, and during busy tourist seasons, it's normal for prices to be higher.

Most foreign passengers arrive in Brazil via the main international airports in cities like São Paulo, Rio de Janeiro, and Brasília. From these hubs, you may simply connect to domestic flights to reach your selected locations inside the country.

Public Transportation

Brazil's cities provide a range of public transit choices to assist you traverse the urban environment effectively. Here are some popular public transit alternatives you'll find in large cities:

- **Metro/Subway:** Cities like São Paulo, Rio de Janeiro, and Brasília have sophisticated metro systems that give a rapid and effective way to navigate the city. Metros are normally safe and well-maintained, making them a popular alternative for residents and visitors alike.

- **Buses:** Brazil's cities have large bus networks that serve most communities and locations. Buses are a cost-effective means of transportation and look at local life. However, they might become congested during peak hours, so be careful with your valuables.

- **Trains and Trams:** Some cities, such as Rio de Janeiro and Belo Horizonte, have railway and tram services that link different areas of the city. These services might be a fascinating way to explore specific locations.

Public transit is a wonderful alternative for commuting inside cities, but it may not always be the most practical choice for distant or rural areas.

Renting a Car

Renting a vehicle in Brazil might be a terrific alternative if you want the flexibility to explore at your leisure, particularly if you want to visit more distant places or prefer not to depend on public transit. Renting a vehicle also enables you to enjoy picturesque drives across Brazil's magnificent landscapes.

Most major cities in Brazil feature international vehicle rental businesses like Hertz, Avis, and Europcar, as well as local companies. To hire a vehicle, you'll need a valid driver's license from your home country and an international driving permit (IDP). The minimum age for renting a vehicle in Brazil is normally 21 years, however, certain rental businesses may demand drivers to be at least 25 years old.

It's necessary to be informed of the driving conditions in Brazil. Traffic in big cities may be crowded and chaotic, while road conditions in rural regions may vary. It's suggested to travel during daytime hours and avoid driving at night in more distant places owing to possible safety problems.

Taxis and Ride-Sharing

Taxis are commonly accessible in major Brazilian cities and are a suitable alternative for short excursions inside metropolitan regions. Taxis may be hailed on the street or obtained at authorized taxi stops. Ensure that the taxi has a functional meter, or negotiate the fee before commencing your trip.

In recent years, ride-sharing services like Uber and 99 have grown more popular in Brazil's cities. These services provide a safe and typically more cheap alternative to regular taxis. Just ensure you have internet connectivity to utilize the app for booking a ride.

When utilizing cabs or ride-sharing services, it's usually a good idea to share your trip information with a friend or family member, particularly if you are going alone.

Traveling Between Cities

Traveling between cities in Brazil may be an experience in itself, with a choice of transportation alternatives to select from:

- **Long-Distance Buses:** Brazil has a large and efficient long-distance bus network run by numerous operators. Buses are a popular alternative for commuting between cities and provide a cost-effective method to view the countryside. The buses are normally pleasant and equipped with air conditioning, and some even feature reclining seats for long travels.

- **Domestic Flights:** As indicated previously, air travel is a wonderful choice for traveling big distances swiftly. Domestic flights link major cities and famous tourist attractions, making it easier to jump from one area to another.

- **Train Travel:** While not as widespread as buses or aircraft, Brazil does offer several picturesque train lines, notably in the Southern area. The Serra Verde Express in Paraná and the Maria Fumaça railway in Minas Gerais are famed for their magnificent scenery.

When arranging your journey between cities, consider the distance, travel duration, and budget. Buses are good for individuals who prefer beautiful travels and have more time, while aircraft provide convenience and time-saving advantages.

Safety Tips for Travelers

Traveling in Brazil, like any other nation, needs some understanding of safety issues and safeguards. While Brazil is a generally safe nation for tourists, it's vital to take some steps to guarantee a pleasant and secure trip:

- **Stay Informed:** Before going to any location, check for any travel warnings or safety alerts issued by your government. Stay educated about local circumstances and possible threats.

- **Avoid Flashy Displays of Wealth:** As a visitor, it's preferable to avoid flaunting costly jewelry, devices, or big quantities of cash in public. Stay cautious in crowded situations to avoid pickpocketing.

- **Choose Reliable Transportation:** When utilizing taxis or ride-sharing services, only choose licensed and reputed providers. Avoid hailing strange cabs on the street, particularly at night.

- **Keep Valuables Secure:** Store your passport, money, and other valuables in a secure and discreet area, such as a hotel safe or a hidden money belt.

- **Respect Local Customs:** Familiarize oneself with local customs and traditions to show respect for the culture and prevent inadvertent misunderstandings.

- **Be Cautious at Night:** While large cities are typically safe, practice caution while wandering alone at night, particularly in poorly lit or unknown regions.

- **Stay in Safe Areas:** Choose hotels in safe and well-reviewed areas, and ask your hotel for guidance on local safety.

- **Avoid High-Crime Locations:** Research the locations you want to visit and avoid neighborhoods renowned for high crime rates.

Getting around Brazil is an experience in itself, with varied transportation alternatives to suit different interests and travel demands. From domestic aircraft that link major cities to long-distance buses that take you through the magnificent countryside, Brazil provides a variety of transportation alternatives for any tourist. Whether you're exploring the metropolitan landscapes, immersing yourself in the Amazon jungle, or visiting the quaint villages of the South, being knowledgeable about transportation alternatives and safety measures will guarantee a smooth and pleasant vacation in this beautiful and varied nation.

TOP DESTINATIONS IN BRAZIL

Brazil is a country abounding with unique attractions and enchanting sites that appeal to a broad variety of interests. From dynamic cities with rich cultural attractions to spectacular natural beauties, Brazil offers something to enchant every tourist. Here are some of the top locations you should consider experiencing during your stay in Brazil:

Rio de Janeiro

Rio de Janeiro, frequently referred to as the "Cidade Maravilhosa" (Marvelous City), is one of Brazil's most renowned locations. This busy town is recognized for its magnificent beaches, vibrant atmosphere, and awe-inspiring monuments.

Christ the Redeemer

Christ the Redeemer, perched atop Corcovado Mountain, is one of the most iconic and identifiable icons of Brazil. This huge statue of Jesus Christ with spread arms gives a panoramic perspective of Rio de Janeiro, making it a great position to shoot magnificent images of the city below.

To reach the monument, guests may take a picturesque train trip through Tijuca National Park or trek along well-marked paths for a more adventurous experience. Watching the dawn or sunset from Christ the Redeemer is a magnificent experience and a highlight of every vacation to Rio de Janeiro.

Copacabana Beach

Copacabana Beach is a renowned expanse of sand that runs over 4 kilometers along the Atlantic coast. This landmark beach is recognized for its busy environment, bright seaside vendors, and magnificent views of the surrounding mountains.

Visitors may enjoy a leisurely walk down the beach, soak up the sun, and indulge in different water sports such as swimming and beach volleyball. In the evening, Copacabana comes alive with beach parties, live music, and a bustling street scene that goes into the night.

Sugarloaf Mountain

Sugarloaf Mountain (Pão de Açúcar) is another renowned feature of Rio de Janeiro. Rising 396 meters above the port, it gives a stunning 360-degree view of the city, Guanabara Bay, and the surrounding mountains.

To reach the peak of Sugarloaf, travelers ride two cable cars, with the first transporting them to Morro da Urca and the second to the summit. Sunset views from Sugarloaf Mountain are especially breathtaking and give a fantastic chance to witness Rio's magnificent city lights come to life.

São Paulo

As Brazil's biggest city and commercial engine, São Paulo is a busy metropolis recognized for its lively culture, rich food scene, and spectacular architecture.

Ibirapuera Park

Ibirapuera Park is an urban oasis in the center of São Paulo, giving a calm getaway from the city's hustle and bustle. The park contains vast green fields, lovely flowers, and various walking and running pathways. It is a popular area for residents and tourists alike to enjoy picnics, outdoor music, and cultural activities.

Within the park, you'll discover different cultural institutions, such as the São Paulo Museum of Modern Art (MAM) and the Afro-Brazil Museum, which display Brazil's rich creative and cultural legacy.

Avenida Paulista

Avenida Paulista is São Paulo's most recognized boulevard and a symbol of the city's economic and cultural vibrancy. The road is flanked by stunning buildings, retail malls, restaurants, and cultural organizations, making it a dynamic and exciting location to visit.

Avenida Paulista is also home to the São Paulo Art Museum (MASP), which has a vast collection of European and Brazilian art, including works by prominent painters such as Van Gogh, Picasso, and Portinari.

Museu de Arte de São Paulo (MASP)

The São Paulo Art Museum (MASP) is one of the most prominent art museums in Brazil and is situated on Avenida Paulista. The museum's distinctive architectural style, with a suspended structure and enormous glass exterior, makes it an architectural wonder.

Inside, MASP exhibits an extraordinary collection of European and Brazilian art from different centuries, including paintings, sculptures, and decorative arts. The museum also holds temporary exhibits and cultural activities, making it a must-visit location for art fans.

Salvador

Salvador, the capital of the state of Bahia, is a bustling city with a rich cultural legacy and a compelling Afro-Brazilian influence. From its colorful streets to its vibrant festivals, Salvador provides a unique and captivating experience for tourists.

Pelourinho Historic Center

Pelourinho is the ancient core of Salvador and a UNESCO World Heritage site. This quaint area is noted for its wonderfully maintained colonial architecture, cobblestone lanes, and colorful pastel-colored houses.

Strolling around Pelourinho, tourists may immerse themselves in the city's history and culture. The region is home to various churches, museums, and cultural institutes, including the São Francisco Church and Convent and the Afro-Brazilian Museum.

In the evening, Pelourinho comes alive with the sounds of traditional music, dance performances, and bustling street parties, making it a perfect site to experience the dynamic atmosphere of Salvador.

Porto da Barra Beach

Porto do Barra Beach is one of Salvador's most popular and attractive beaches. Located in the Barra district, the beach has calm waves, making it excellent for swimming and water sports.

The beach is surrounded by cafés and restaurants, where tourists may sample wonderful Bahian food and cool beverages while enjoying breathtaking views of the ocean. Porto do Barra is also an excellent site to observe the sunset over the Atlantic horizon.

Mercado Modelo

Mercado Modelo, situated along the shore, is one of Salvador's most renowned marketplaces. Housed in a historic structure, the market is a treasure trove of handicrafts, souvenirs, and local items.

Here, you may discover a broad selection of things, including traditional Bahian arts & crafts, apparel, jewelry, and spices. It's a fantastic spot to pick up unique presents and immerse yourself in the local culture.

Manaus

Manaus, the capital of the state of Amazonas, is a gateway to the Amazon rainforest and a city rich in history and natural beauty. Nestled in the beautiful jungle, Manaus provides a wonderful mix of civilization and environment.

Amazon Rainforest Tours

One of the primary attractions of Manaus is the possibility to go on Amazon jungle excursions. Various tour providers offer trips into the huge and biodiverse jungle, enabling tourists to enjoy its natural treasures up close.

During these trips, you may explore the deep forest, view rare creatures, and learn about the unique ecology of the Amazon. Some excursions also include visits to indigenous villages, allowing an insight into their traditional way of life.

Meeting of the Waters

The Meeting of the Waters is a beautiful natural occurrence that happens in Manaus. Here, the black waters of the Rio Negro and the sandy-colored waters of the Rio Solimões run side by side for many kilometers without mingling, providing a dramatic contrast in hues.

The two rivers ultimately join to create the gigantic Amazon River, the biggest river in the world by discharge volume. Witnessing magnificent natural phenomena is a must-do experience for tourists to Manaus.

Teatro Amazonas (Amazon Theatre)

The Teatro Amazonas, popularly known as the Amazon Theatre, is an architectural jewel and an iconic emblem of Manaus. This vast opera building, created during the rubber boom period, features exquisite neo-Renaissance and Belle Époque architecture.

Visitors may take guided tours of the theater to appreciate its sumptuous interiors, featuring a dome covered with 36,000 ceramic tiles symbolizing the Brazilian national flag. The Amazon Theatre continues to offer numerous cultural events, including concerts, ballet performances, and opera presentations.

Florianópolis

Florianópolis, the capital of the state of Santa Catarina, is a lovely island city noted for its magnificent beaches, lively culture, and outdoor sports. With its ideal combination of urban life and natural beauty, Florianópolis has become a popular destination for vacationers seeking both rest and adventure.

Praia Mole

Praia Mole is one of Florianópolis' most recognized and popular beaches, drawing both residents and visitors alike. This lengthy stretch of golden sand is bordered by beautiful hills and crystal-clear seas, making it a great site for swimming, surfing, and sunbathing.

The beach's laid-back vibe and beachfront bars make it a favorite among the younger demographic. Praia Mole regularly organizes international surfing events, inviting surfers from across the globe to enjoy its famed waves.

Lagoa da Conceição

Lagoa da Conceição is a lovely lagoon situated in the center of the island. Surrounded by dunes and verdant hills, the lagoon provides a beautiful backdrop for numerous water sports, such as stand-up paddleboarding, kayaking, and sailing.

The region near Lagoa da Conceição is also renowned for its active nightlife, with various clubs, restaurants, and live music venues. It's a terrific spot to experience the local food and immerse yourself in the city's vibrant environment.

Ilha do Campeche

Ilha do Campeche, popularly known as Campeche Island, is a virgin island situated just off the coast of Florianópolis. Accessible only by boat, this island is a protected natural reserve, providing tourists a chance to explore unspoiled beaches, stroll through lush woods, and uncover old rock inscriptions left by early residents.

The island is a popular destination for snorkeling and scuba diving since its pristine waters are home to rich marine life and vivid coral reefs. With minimal daily visits permitted, Ilha do Campeche preserves its unspoiled beauty and tranquility.

Brasília

Brasília, the capital of Brazil, is a city recognized for its modernist architecture, futuristic design, and political importance. Designed by famous architect Oscar Niemeyer and urban planner Lúcio Costa, Brasília is a UNESCO World Heritage site and a living testament to modernist architecture and urban design.

Three Powers Plaza

The Three Powers Plaza, or Praça dos Três Poderes, is the core of Brazil's political power and a must-visit attraction in Brasília. This huge plaza is bordered by three key government buildings: the Palácio do Planalto (Presidential Palace), the National Congress, and the Supreme Federal Court.

The plaza's famous design, with Niemeyer's unique architecture and sculptures by renowned artist Bruno Giorgi, depicts the three branches of government working peacefully to administer the country.

Palácio do Planalto

The Palácio do Planalto, often known as the Planalto Palace, is the official workplace and house of the President of Brazil. The building's sleek lines and spectacular design reflect the modernist elements that distinguish Brasília's architecture.

While the inside is not normally available to the public, visitors may nevertheless appreciate the building's front and explore the surrounding gardens and squares.

Cathedral of Brasília

The Cathedral of Brasília, formally titled Catedral Metropolitana Nossa Senhora Aparecida, is another prominent architectural masterpiece in the city. Designed by Oscar Niemeyer, the cathedral's unusual hyperboloid form with its glass roof allows for an abundance of natural light, providing a tranquil and spiritual ambiance.

Inside, visitors may marvel at the stunning 14-meter-high bronze statues of the four evangelists and the beautiful stained glass panels that flood the interior in a fascinating palette of hues.

Brazil provides a surprising assortment of great locations, each delivering a combination of exciting city life, spectacular natural beauty, and rich cultural experiences. From the renowned Christ the Redeemer in Rio de Janeiro to the busy Avenida Paulista in São Paulo, tourists are treated to remarkable encounters. Salvador's Pelourinho Historic Center takes tourists to Brazil's colonial history and Afro-Brazilian culture, while Manaus opens doors to the awe-inspiring Amazon jungle.

The Amazon Theatre lends a touch of refinement to the Manaus experience. Florianópolis satisfies with gorgeous beaches and lagoons, appealing to beach lovers and explorers alike. In contrast, Brasília's modernist architecture and significant government buildings symbolize Brazil's progressive attitude. Whether experiencing Salvador's bustling streets or basking in the delights of Brasília, these sites provide distinct and fascinating experiences of an amazing tour across enthralling Brazil.

OFF-THE-BEATEN-PATH DESTINATIONS IN BRAZIL

While Brazil's popular attractions like Rio de Janeiro and São Paulo are recognized globally, the country is also home to several hidden treasures and off-the-beaten-path spots that provide unique and memorable experiences. From beautiful colonial villages to spectacular natural marvels, these lesser-known sites are great for tourists wishing to experience the hidden gems of Brazil. Let's look into some of these hidden gems:

Paraty

Located along Brazil's Costa Verde (Green Coast), Paraty is a lovely colonial town with a rich history and natural beauty. The town's well-preserved buildings and cobblestone streets ooze an old-world charm, making it a favored destination for history fans and architectural enthusiasts.

Paraty is also bordered by beautiful tropical woods and lovely beaches, adding to its charm. The location provides a plethora of outdoor activities, including hiking, boat cruises to adjacent islands, and kayaking along the peaceful waters of Paraty Bay.

One of the attractions of Paraty is the annual Paraty International Literary Festival (FLIP), which gathers famous writers and literary aficionados from across the globe. The festival brings the town to life with literary debates, readings, and cultural activities.

Lençóis Maranhenses National Park

Tucked away in the state of Maranhão, Lençóis Maranhenses National Park is a weird and otherworldly site. This unusual park has enormous areas of dunes studded with lagoons of crystal-clear freshwater, providing a magnificent visual contrast against the blue sky.

The greatest time to visit Lençóis Maranhenses is during the rainy season (between February and June) when the lagoons are at their largest. Exploring the park's strange terrain and enjoying a cool plunge into the lagoons is an astonishing experience that seems like walking into a dream.

Bonito

Bonito, situated in the state of Mato Grosso do Sul, is a hidden treasure famed for its crystal-clear rivers, waterfalls, and distinctive limestone formations. The region's eco-tourism emphasis assures sustainable and ethical tourism, making it a fantastic alternative for nature enthusiasts and adventure seekers.

One of the attractions of Bonito is snorkeling or scuba diving in the Rio da Prata and Rio Sucuri, where tourists may experience an astonishing underwater environment rich with colorful fish and beautiful aquatic vegetation. The neighboring Blue Lagoon Cave (Gruta do Lago Azul) is a natural beauty with a deep, brilliant blue lagoon at its foot.

Bonito also provides hiking possibilities, birding, and exploring natural sinkholes known as "cenotes." The region's conservation efforts and magnificent scenery make it a must-visit destination for anyone seeking a pure and real nature experience.

Jericoacoara

Jericoacoara, popularly referred to as "Jeri," is a secluded and picturesque fishing community tucked on the northeastern coast of Brazil. With its laid-back ambiance and magnificent beaches, Jericoacoara is an excellent location for those seeking tranquility and natural beauty.

The region's most prominent attraction is the Jericoacoara National Park, which has dunes, mangroves, and lagoons. The dunes give good prospects for sandboarding, while the lagoons provide a pleasant getaway from the tropical heat.

Jericoacoara is also a known destination for windsurfing and kitesurfing owing to its constant winds and great conditions. Watching the sunset from the huge dune known as "Duna do Pôr do Sol" is a wonderful experience and a treasured memory for many people.

Chapada Diamantina

Chapada Diamantina, situated in the center of Bahia, is a huge and rocky territory noted by its breathtaking scenery, subterranean caverns, and soothing waterfalls. This hidden treasure is a refuge for hikers, trekkers, and wildlife aficionados.

The region's diversified topography includes table-top mountains, verdant valleys, and stunning rock formations. Some of the must-visit locations are the Pai Inácio Hill, where tourists can see stunning panoramic views, and the Poço Encantado and Poço Azul, two hypnotic subterranean lakes.

Chapada Diamantina is also a heaven for adventure lovers, providing options for canyoning, rappelling, and cave exploring. The region's natural beauty and adventurous attitude make it a memorable location for those wishing to connect with nature.

Ouro Preto

Ouro Preto, situated in the state of Minas Gerais, is a UNESCO World Heritage-listed village that transports tourists back in time to Brazil's colonial past. The town's well-preserved architecture and cobblestone streets are a tribute to its long history and cultural value.

Ouro Preto's ancient churches, such as the São Francisco de Assis Church and Nossa Senhora do Pilar Church, are excellent specimens of baroque architecture and contain outstanding pieces of art. The town's art and music culture also contribute to its cultural attractiveness.

Beyond its colonial legacy, Ouro Preto is surrounded by spectacular natural settings, making it a wonderful location for trekking and exploring the local waterfalls and mountains.

Brazil's hidden jewels and off-the-beaten-path sites provide a plethora of unique and fascinating experiences for tourists. From the beautiful colonial village of Paraty to the strange landscapes of Lençóis Maranhenses National Park and the pure beauty of Bonito, these sites enable tourists to engage with Brazil's vast natural and cultural history in a more personal and genuine manner.

BRAZILIAN CUISINE

Must-Try Brazilian Dishes

Brazilian cuisine is a fascinating combination of tastes and influences, reflecting the country's broad cultural background and plentiful natural resources. From robust meat meals to tropical fruits and exquisite desserts, here are seven must-try Brazilian cuisineS that will excite your taste buds:

1. Feijoada

Considered Brazil's national meal, feijoada is a thick and savory stew cooked with black beans and a range of pig and beef pieces. Served with rice, collard greens, orange slices, and farofa (toasted cassava flour), feijoada is a robust and fulfilling dish often savored on Saturdays.

2. Pão de Queijo

These little, chewy cheese bread rolls are a favorite Brazilian snack or morning delight. Made with tapioca flour and cheese, pão de queijo has a wonderful cheesy flavor and a soft, doughy texture that makes them tempting.

3. Moqueca

Moqueca is a classic Brazilian fish stew cooked with coconut milk, tomatoes, onions, garlic, and other herbs and spices. The meal is cooked gently, enabling the flavors to mingle together, resulting in a rich and aromatic seafood delicacy.

4. Coxinha

A popular street meal, coxinha is a deep-fried pastry stuffed with shredded chicken and cream cheese. The dough is formed like a teardrop or drumstick, earning it the Portuguese name "coxinha," which translates to "little thigh."

5. Churrasco

Brazil is famed for its churrasco, a delectable barbeque style of food. Various pieces of meat, such as picanha (top sirloin cap) and fraldinha (flank steak), are seasoned with rock salt and grilled over an open flame, resulting in soft and tasty meats.

6. Açaí Bowl

A pleasant and healthful treat, açaí bowls are created with frozen açaí berries combined into a thick and creamy smoothie. The dish is then topped with granola, fresh fruits, and occasionally honey or condensed milk.

Regional Specialties

Brazil's large size and geographical variety have given birth to a broad assortment of regional specialties, each with its tastes and ingredients. Here is some regional cuisine you should seek out:

1. Acarajé (Salvador, Bahia)

This meal is a famous street snack in Salvador, made with deep-fried black-eyed pea fritters stuffed with spicy shrimp and different seasonings.

2. Barreado (Paraná)

A traditional cuisine from the state of Paraná, barreado is a slow-cooked beef stew seasoned with spices and eaten with cassava flour.

3. Baião de Dois (Northeast)

Hailing from the Northeast area, baião de dois is a savory meal composed of rice, beans, cheese, and occasionally pork or dried beef.

4. Tacacá (North)

A popular cuisine in the Amazon area, tacacá is a savory soup cooked with tucupi (a yellow sauce produced from manioc), jambu leaves, shrimp, and spices.

Popular Restaurants and Food Markets

Brazil provides a bustling culinary scene with restaurants and food markets catering to a varied variety of tastes and preferences. Here are some popular eating venues to explore:

1. Mercado Municipal (São Paulo): São Paulo's Mercado Municipal is a food market bursting with booths selling a broad range of fresh vegetables, meats, cheeses, and local specialties. Don't miss sampling the legendary mortadella sandwich, a great gourmet pleasure.

2. Comida Mineira Restaurantes (Minas Gerais): In Minas Gerais, indulge in comida mineira, the typical food of the area. Look for family-owned eateries that offer foods like tutu de feijão (a bean and pig stew), pão de queijo, and doce de leite (a caramel-like milk dessert).

3. Feira de São Cristóvão (Rio de Janeiro): This vibrant market in Rio de Janeiro promotes northeastern food and culture. Sample regional delicacies, see live music performances, and enjoy the colorful ambiance of Brazil's northeastern area.

4. Maní (São Paulo): For a superb dining experience that exhibits Brazilian tastes with a modern touch, visit Maní in São Paulo. The restaurant is noted for its unique meals influenced by Brazilian ingredients and culinary traditions.

5. Restaurante Chão Nativo (Cuiabá, Mato Grosso): If you find yourself in Cuiabá, Mato Grosso, travel to Restaurante Chão Nativo to experience real cuiabano meals, including dishes using local seafood and the famed lamb stew.

Brazilian food is a delicious blend of varied influences, and studying the country's must-try dishes, regional specialties, and renowned eating venues is a gastronomic trip that will leave you with a better understanding of Brazil's rich culinary legacy. Whether you're relishing the classic feijoada, delighting in the tropical aromas of açaí bowls, or finding regional specialties at local markets, Brazil's culinary pleasures are guaranteed to impress and please any pallet.

CULTURAL EXPERIENCES

Carnival in Brazil

Carnival is one of Brazil's most famous and lively cultural events, celebrated with grandiosity and passion across the nation. This yearly event takes place in the days preceding Lent, generally in February or March, and draws millions of tourists from across the globe.

Rio de Janeiro's Carnival is undoubtedly the most renowned, with its grandiose samba parades with bright floats, flamboyant costumes, and samba schools fighting for top awards. The Sambadrome, a purpose-built parade arena, provides the scene for this magnificent show of music, dancing, and culture.

Other cities like Salvador and Recife also have exciting Carnivals with distinct customs. Salvador's Carnival is notable for its trio elétrico (electric truck) parades, where artists sing and dance atop rolling trucks, creating a pulsing street party.

During Carnival, visitors may immerse themselves in Brazilian culture by attending street parties known as "blocos," where residents and tourists dance to rhythmic music, donning costumes and engaging in the cheerful mood of the celebrations.

Capoeira and Brazilian Martial Arts

Capoeira is a unique and captivating martial art that developed in Brazil during the colonial era. Developed by enslaved Africans as a means of self-defense, capoeira is a combination of acrobatics, dance, and martial arts maneuvers accompanied by rhythmic music and singing.

Today, capoeira is not only practiced as a combat art but also as a form of cultural expression and fellowship. Visitors may watch mesmerizing capoeira performances in public parks, beaches, and plazas, where practitioners, known as "capoeiristas," demonstrate their agility and talent in a circle called a "roda."

Participating in a capoeira class or roda is a chance to not only learn the martial art but also get insights into the historical and cultural relevance of this interesting Brazilian culture.

Samba and Forró Dance

Samba and Forró are two prominent Brazilian dance forms that show the country's enthusiasm for music and movement.

Samba is not just a dance but also a musical genre that developed in the favelas (slums) of Rio de Janeiro. It has now become an intrinsic element of Brazilian identity and culture. Visitors may enjoy samba in numerous ways, from taking samba dance courses to visiting live performances in pubs and clubs.

Forró is another traditional dance form that developed in Northeastern Brazil, mainly in the states of Pernambuco and Ceará. Forró comprises vibrant music performed with accordion, zabumba (bass drum), and triangle. The dance is characterized by intimate partner dancing with whirling and rhythmic footwork.

Participating in a samba or forró dance night in Brazil enables tourists to immerse themselves in the country's lively dance culture and engage with locals who are always willing to share their enthusiasm for dancing.

Indigenous Culture and Communities

Brazil is home to several indigenous populations, each with its particular customs, dialects, and cultural practices. Visiting these villages gives a unique chance to learn about the country's indigenous history and its profound connection to the land.

In the Amazon area, travelers might meet tribes such as the Yanomami, Kayapó, and Tikuna, among others. Many communities allow tourists to experience their way of life, engage in ceremonies, and learn about their traditional knowledge of medicinal herbs and ecological methods.

Tour companies and local groups provide ethical and sustainable ecotourism experiences, offering tourists the ability to help indigenous people while receiving insight into their rich cultural history.

Religious Festivals and Traditions

Religion has a prominent part in Brazilian society, and religious holidays and rituals are observed with zeal and dedication.

One such event is Festa de Iemanjá, devoted to the Afro-Brazilian god of the sea and water. Celebrated on February 2nd, devotees dressed in white and present gifts like flowers and jewels, which are sent out to sea as offerings to Iemanjá.

Semana Santa (Holy Week) leading up to Easter is also a prominent religious holiday in Brazil, highlighted by processions, religious services, and reenactments of the Passion of Christ in numerous cities and villages.

In the northeastern area, the celebration of São João (Saint John) during June is a vivid and colorful occasion. Festivities include bonfires, traditional dances, and a variety of native delicacies prepared with maize, such as canjica and pamonha.

Participating in these religious festivals and customs gives tourists a look into the spiritual and cultural components of Brazil, and a chance to observe the deep faith and variety of the Brazilian people.

Brazil provides a rich tapestry of cultural experiences that enable tourists to interact with the country's past, customs, and dynamic spirit. Whether it's joining the exuberant festivities of Carnival, learning the rhythmic movements of capoeira, dancing to the beats of samba and forró, engaging with indigenous communities, or participating in religious festivals, these cultural experiences provide a deeper understanding of Brazil's cultural diversity and the warmth of its people.

OUTDOOR ACTIVITIES & ADVENTURE

Beach Activities and Water Sports

Brazil's enormous coastline, ranging nearly 7,400 kilometers, provides a variety of beach activities and water sports. From resting on immaculate sandy coastlines to exhilarating aquatic experiences, Brazil's beaches appeal to all sorts of tourists. Here are some of the best beach activities and water sports to enjoy in Brazil:

- **Beach Bumming:** Whether it's the legendary Copacabana in Rio de Janeiro, the serene Porto de Galinhas in Pernambuco, or the beautiful Praia do Farol in Arraial do Cabo, Brazil's beaches are excellent for soaking up the sun, building sandcastles, and enjoying refreshing swims in the water.

- **Beach Volleyball:** Beach volleyball is a popular activity in Brazil, and you'll frequently see residents and visitors playing spontaneous matches on the sandy shoreline. Join in the fun or just watch the experts exhibit their abilities.

- **Stand-Up Paddleboarding (SUP):** Stand-up paddleboarding has gained popularity in Brazil, and it's a fantastic opportunity to explore calm seas, lagoons, and mangroves while getting a workout. Locations like Lagoa da Conceição in Florianópolis and Lagoa Rodrigo de Freitas in Rio de Janeiro are suitable for SUP excursions.

- **Kite Flying:** Kite flying is a common hobby on Brazilian beaches, particularly during windy days. Join the locals as they fly their multicolored kites into the sky, creating a brilliant show.

- **Beach Soccer:** Brazil's enthusiasm for soccer extends to the beaches, where you can frequently see spontaneous beach soccer matches. Join the locals for a casual game or cheer from the sidelines.

Hiking in National Parks

Brazil is home to multiple national parks, giving wonderful chances for hiking and trekking lovers to discover the country's unique landscapes and ecosystems. Some of the top hiking and trekking sites include:

- **Chapada Diamantina National Park:** Located in Bahia, Chapada Diamantina has breathtaking table-top mountains, crystal-clear rivers, and gorgeous waterfalls. The park provides different routes, including the classic walk to the summit of Pai Inácio Hill for stunning panoramic views.

- **Iguazu National Park:** On the border with Argentina, Iguazu National Park provides awe-inspiring walks through the thick jungle up to the famed Iguazu Falls. The park's vast path network enables visitors to experience numerous vistas of the beautiful waterfalls.

- **Chapada dos Veadeiros National Park:** This park in the state of Goiás contains spectacular canyons, waterfalls, and unusual rock formations. Hiking to the viewpoint spots affords breathtaking panoramas of the Cerrado ecosystem.

- **Tijuca National Park:** Located inside Rio de Janeiro, Tijuca National Park is one of the world's biggest urban woods. Trails lead to vistas, such as Pedra Bonita and Pedra da Gávea, where tourists may enjoy beautiful views of the city and coastline.

- **Lençóis Maranhenses National Park:** Although famed for its dunes and lagoons, Lençóis Maranhenses also provides exhilarating hikes through the dunes to secluded lagoons during the wet season.

Wildlife Watching and Eco-Tours

Brazil's various ecosystems give many possibilities for animal observation and eco-tours. Here are some of the greatest spots to see the country's tremendous biodiversity:

- **The Pantanal:** The Pantanal, the world's biggest tropical wetland, is a nature lover's heaven. Embark on eco-tours and boat safaris to observe jaguars, caimans, gigantic otters, and a multitude of bird species.

- **Amazon Rainforest:** The Amazon rainforest is rich with species, from brilliant macaws to elusive jaguars and lively river dolphins. Guided forest hikes and boat tours provide amazing experiences with the region's vegetation and animals.

- **Fernando de Noronha:** This archipelago is a UNESCO World Heritage site and a sanctuary for aquatic life. Snorkeling and diving here allow swimming among marine turtles, dolphins, and sharks.

- **Reserva Ecológica de Guapiaçu:** Located in Rio de Janeiro state, this reserve is a birdwatcher's delight, home to hundreds of bird species, including toucans, parrots, and the stunning Harpy Eagle.

- **Pantanal Jaguar Safaris:** Organized trips in the Pantanal concentrate on following and studying the elusive jaguars in their natural environment. These safaris give unique and exhilarating opportunities to observe these majestic big cats up close.

Surfing and Kitesurfing Spots

Brazil's coastline is lined with outstanding surfing and kitesurfing areas, drawing water sports aficionados from across the globe. Some of the top surf and kitesurf spots include:

- **Itacaré:** This laid-back town in Bahia is famed for its stunning beaches and steady waves, making it a favorite among surfers.

- **Florianópolis:** Known as the "Island of Magic," Florianópolis features various surf locations catering to all ability levels, including the legendary Joaquina Beach.

- **Praia do Rosa:** This picturesque beach in Santa Catarina is not only a famous surf area but also an excellent site to observe migratory whales during certain months of the year.

- **Jericoacoara:** Jericoacoara, or "Jeri," provides great conditions for kitesurfing, with strong and steady winds and magnificent dunes.

- **Barra Grande:** Located near Piauí, Barra Grande is a hidden treasure for kitesurfing, with shallow and warm seas, making it excellent for beginners and expert riders alike.

Scuba Diving and Snorkeling

Brazil's coastal waters are filled with marine life, making it a superb location for scuba diving and snorkeling. Some of the best sites for underwater exploration include:

- **Fernando de Noronha:** This archipelago is a marine protected area, providing crystal-clear seas and exceptional visibility for both snorkelers and divers. Encounter marine turtles, sharks, and schools of colorful fish.

- **Abrolhos:** Abrolhos Marine National Park is a refuge for scuba divers, particularly between July and November when humpback whales travel through the area.

- **Bonito:** While noted for its freshwater features, Bonito also provides snorkeling chances in the crystal-clear waters of the Rio da Prata and Rio Sucuri.

- **Maracajaú:** Located in Rio Grande do Norte, Maracajaú is home to natural coral formations called "Parrachos," giving a magnificent snorkeling experience.

- **Ilha Grande:** This island off the coast of Rio de Janeiro features various diving sites with abundant marine species and the potential to encounter rays, turtles, and even shipwrecks.

Brazil's vast and varied landscapes offer a playground for outdoor lovers and adventure seekers. Whether you're resting on the sandy beaches, trekking through national parks, viewing animals in the Pantanal, catching waves in the Atlantic, or discovering the undersea marvels, Brazil provides a multitude of thrilling and memorable outdoor activities for tourists of all ages and interests. From the Amazon jungle to the beautiful beaches, Brazil's natural beauty lures travelers to go on adventurous activities and leave lasting memories in this enchanting nation.

BRAZIL'S RICH WILDLIFE

The Amazon Rainforest and its wildlife

The Amazon Rainforest is one of the most biodiverse ecosystems on the globe, and its fauna is nothing short of astounding. Spanning over nine nations, Brazil is home to the greatest area of the Amazon Rainforest, which occupies nearly 60% of its land. Here are some of the magnificent animal species present in this rich and diversified ecosystem:

- **Jaguar (Panthera onca):** The jaguar, the biggest big cat in the Americas, is a symbol of power and stealth. It roams the deep Amazon jungle and is a top predator in the area.

- **Harpy Eagle (Harpia harpyja):** With its stunning appearance and formidable claws, the harpy eagle is one of the most remarkable and elusive raptors found in the Amazon. It preys on monkeys and sloths, employing its remarkable vision and hunting abilities.

- **Pink River Dolphin (Inia geoffrensis):** The lovely pink river dolphin is a rare species found in the Amazon River and its tributaries. Known for their pink color, they are very clever and gregarious animals.

- **Giant Otter (Pteronura brasiliensis):** The giant otter is the biggest of its type and may be found swimming in the Amazon's rivers. These lively and very gregarious creatures are outstanding hunters, frequently observed capturing fish in groups.

- **Poison Dart Frogs:** The Amazon is home to a spectacular collection of brilliantly colored poison dart frogs. While their brilliant colors are enticing, they contain strong poisons to discourage predators.

Pantanal Wetlands

The Pantanal is the world's biggest tropical wetland and is commonly referred to as South America's animal paradise. It is situated in the states of Mato Grosso and Mato Grosso do Sul in Brazil. The Pantanal is recognized for its amazing biodiversity and is a UNESCO World Heritage site. Some of the animal species discovered in this particular habitat include:

- **Giant Anteater (Myrmecophaga tridactyla):** The Pantanal is an excellent site to observe these remarkable species, famed for their large snouts and huge tongues, employed to suck up ants and termites.

- **Giant River Otter (Pteronura brasiliensis):** Similar to their Amazonian relatives, giant river otters flourish in the Pantanal's streams. They are very gregarious creatures and commonly found in family groupings.

- **Hyacinth Macaw (Anodorhynchus hyacinthinus):** The brilliant blue hyacinth macaw is one of the biggest parrots in the world and is endemic to the Pantanal. Its stunning look and lively activity make it a favorite species for birdwatchers.

- **Jabiru Stork (Jabiru mycteria):** The jabiru stork, with its massive size and unique black and white plumage, is a regular sight in the Pantanal. These storks construct their large nests on towering trees and feed on fish and other water critters.

Atlantic Forest Biodiversity

The Atlantic Forest, also known as Mata Atlântica, is a critically vulnerable and biodiverse biosphere situated along Brazil's eastern coast. Despite severe destruction, it remains a hotspot for unusual and endangered species. Some of the fauna found in the Atlantic Forest include:

- **Golden Lion Tamarin (Leontopithecus rosalia):** This little, gorgeous monkey with its golden fur is unique to the Atlantic Forest. Conservation initiatives have helped boost the population of this severely endangered species.

- **South American Tapir (Tapirus terrestris):** The tapir is a big, herbivorous mammal found in the Atlantic Forest and other parts of South America. It serves a critical function in seed distribution and ecosystem preservation.

- **Three-toed Sloth (Bradypus variegatus):** The Atlantic Forest is home to the three-toed sloth, a slow-moving and placid creature that spends much of its time hanging from branches.

- **Harlequin Beetle (Acrocinus longimanus):** This beautiful beetle with its vivid colors and long appendages is one of the distinctive bug species found in the Atlantic Forest.

Birdwatching Hotspots

Brazil is a birdwatcher's dream, with a startling variety of avian species. Birdwatching aficionados will find plenty of sites to visit around the nation. Some of the top spots for birding in Brazil include:

- **Pantanal:** The Pantanal is not only famed for its wildlife but also for its birds. Birdwatchers may observe a large assortment of aquatic birds, including herons, storks, and kingfishers, as well as beautiful macaws and parakeets.

- **Amazon Rainforest:** The Amazon is home to an incredible variety of bird species, from small hummingbirds to magnificent harpy eagles. Birdwatching trips in the Amazon give the possibility to observe rare and unique species.

- **Atlantic Forest:** This biodiverse ecosystem is a delight for birdwatchers, with an astounding diversity of songbirds, tanagers, and toucans.

- **Chapada dos Guimarães National Park:** Located in the state of Mato Grosso, this park is notable for its rich birds, including raptors and vultures.

- **Chapada dos Veadeiros National Park:** Birdwatchers may observe a variety of species in this area, including toucans, parrots, and the spectacular harpy eagle.

Brazil's abundant fauna is a monument to the country's incredible biodiversity and the necessity of protecting its different habitats. From the lush Amazon Rainforest and the colorful Pantanal wetlands to the distinctive Atlantic Forest and its spectacular birding locations, Brazil provides a truly remarkable experience for environment lovers and animal aficionados. Whether you're exploring the thick jungle or viewing colorful birds in their natural environment, these experiences with Brazil's wildlife are guaranteed to create a lasting impact and build greater respect for the country's natural heritage.

TRAVELING WITH SPECIAL INTERESTS

Family-friendly Activities

Brazil is a superb location for family travel, providing a broad selection of activities and sights that appeal to all ages. From the renowned beaches to fascinating animal encounters, here are some family-friendly activities to consider while going to Brazil:

1. Beach Pleasure: Brazil's beaches give countless options for family pleasure. The calm and shallow seas of Porto de Galinhas and Praia do Forte are great for small children to splash about and construct sandcastles. Teens and adults may try their hand at surfing in Florianópolis or kite flying in Fortaleza.

2. Amazon Jungle Trip: Embark on a family-friendly Amazon jungle trip to experience the delights of this unique environment. Guided boat tours and forest hikes enable families to observe amazing wildlife including monkeys, colorful birds, and playful river dolphins.

3. Family-friendly Resorts: Many Brazilian beach locations, such as Porto Seguro and Búzios, have family-friendly resorts with kid's clubs, water parks, and numerous activities geared toward young tourists. These resorts give parents a chance to rest while youngsters have fun.

4. Wildlife Encounters: Head to the Pantanal, where families may engage in exhilarating wildlife excursions. Spotting jaguars, capybaras, and gigantic otters in their natural environment is an amazing experience for both kids and adults.

5. Tijuca National Park: Located in Rio de Janeiro, Tijuca National Park provides family-friendly hiking routes leading to stunning overlooks. Kids will appreciate exploring the jungle and witnessing monkeys swinging among the trees.

6. Rio de Janeiro Botanical Garden: Take a leisurely walk around the Botanical Garden, home to a large assortment of plants and trees, including exotic orchids and towering royal palms.

7. Parque do Mônica (Monica's Park): Located in São Paulo, Parque da Mônica is an amusement park centered on the renowned Brazilian cartoon characters. It includes several rides and attractions appropriate for young children.

8. Beach Volleyball Tournaments: For sports-loving families, watching or even playing in beach volleyball tournaments on renowned beaches like Copacabana or Ipanema in Rio de Janeiro may be a fun and thrilling experience.

LGBTQ+ Travelers' Guide

Brazil is recognized for its dynamic and accepting LGBTQ+ community, making it a friendly destination for LGBTQ+ visitors. While Brazil is largely progressive in its views towards the LGBTQ+ community, it's crucial to keep aware of local norms and practices. Here are some guidelines for LGBTQ+ visitors visiting Brazil:

1. LGBTQ+ Friendly Cities: São Paulo and Rio de Janeiro are two of the most LGBTQ+ friendly cities in Brazil. São Paulo holds one of the biggest LGBTQ+ pride parades in the world.

2. Nightlife: Brazil's nightlife is busy and diversified, featuring LGBTQ+-friendly pubs and clubs in major cities. Lapa in Rio de Janeiro and Rua Augusta in São Paulo are prominent nightlife areas.

3. Safety: While Brazil is usually LGBTQ+ accepting, it's vital to practice care and avoid exhibiting overt love in public, particularly in more traditional places.

4. LGBTQ+ Events: Check the calendar for LGBTQ+ events and festivals, including pride parades and cultural festivities, which take place throughout the year in different locations.

5. Copacabana Beach: In Rio de Janeiro, Copacabana Beach is regarded as a meeting location for the LGBTQ+ community, creating a dynamic and welcoming environment.

6. Supported Lodgings: Many hotels and lodgings in major cities are LGBTQ+ friendly and offer a welcoming atmosphere for all tourists.

7. Embrace Diversity: Brazil's culture promotes diversity, and LGBTQ+ visitors are often welcomed and accepted by locals.

Embrace the country's inclusive attitude and appreciate the friendly welcome.

Solo Travel Tips

Traveling alone in Brazil may be an exciting and freeing experience. However, like any vacation, it's vital to take care and be conscious of your safety. Here are some solo travel suggestions for a smooth and pleasurable vacation in Brazil:

1. Research and Plan: Do comprehensive research about your location, local traditions, and safety advice before your journey. Plan your itinerary and have a basic concept of the sites you'd want to see.

2. Accommodations: Choose accommodations in safe and convenient districts. Hostels may be a terrific choice for lone travelers to meet like-minded folks.

3. Local Transportation: Utilize trustworthy transportation providers and avoid going alone late at night. If you're utilizing public transit, keep a watch on your valuables.

4. Learn Basic Portuguese: While English is spoken in tourist areas, knowing some basic Portuguese phrases can help you converse and explore more successfully.

5. Avoid Flashy Displays: Avoid wearing costly jewelry or showcasing expensive electronics to decrease the danger of drawing unwanted attention.

6. Stay Connected: Keep your family or friends updated about your vacation intentions and share your itinerary with them. Stay engaged with them frequently, particularly in rural places.

7. Group Tours: Consider joining group tours for specific activities, such as hikes or wildlife excursions, where you may meet other visitors and have the help of a guide.

8. Trust Your Instincts: If anything doesn't seem right, trust your instincts and remove yourself from the situation. Be wary when accepting offers from strangers.

9. Travel Insurance: Purchase comprehensive travel insurance that covers medical emergencies and unforeseen occurrences.

Adventure Enthusiast's Itinerary

For adventure fans, Brazil offers a varied choice of adrenaline-pumping activities and exhilarating encounters. Here's an itinerary to fulfill the adventurous soul:

Day 1 - Rio de Janeiro:

- Arrive in Rio de Janeiro and acclimatize to the colorful city.
- Head to Tijuca National Park for a day of trekking, discovering waterfalls, and spotting animals.
- Experience a tandem hang gliding ride from Pedra Bonita for a stunning aerial perspective of Rio's prominent sights.

Day 2 - Rio de Janeiro:

- Enjoy a day of surfing or bodyboarding at Arpoador Beach or Prainha Beach.
- In the evening, enjoy a thrilling Jeep excursion to the summit of Corcovado Mountain for a close-up view of Christ the Redeemer monument.

Day 3 - Ilha Grande:

- Travel to Ilha Grande, a picturesque island noted for its clean beaches and thick vegetation.
- Explore the island's hiking paths, such as the Pico do Papagaio hike, affording panoramic vistas.

Day 4 - Ilha Grande:

- Go snorkeling or scuba diving to experience the diverse marine life in the crystal-clear waters around the island.
- Relax on the beaches and take in the serene ambiance of this tropical paradise.

Day 5 - Bonito:

- Fly to Bonito, a place famed for its crystal-clear rivers and exhilarating eco-adventures.

- Participate in a snorkeling trip in the Rio Sucuri or Rio da Prata to witness colorful fish and underwater life.

Day 6 - Bonito:

- Embark on a fascinating cave exploring experience in Grutas de São Miguel or Abismo Anhumas.
- Enjoy a night snorkeling cruise in the Rio Formoso to witness nocturnal creatures.

Day 7 - Pantanal:

- Travel to the Pantanal, the world's biggest tropical wetland, for a wildlife safari trip.
- Spot jaguars, huge otters, and a multitude of bird species on guided excursions.

Day 8 - Pantanal:

- Continue exploring the Pantanal with activities like horseback riding and boat trips.
- Capture amazing wildlife images throughout your adventures.

Day 9 - Foz do Iguaçu:

- Fly to Foz do Iguaçu to experience the spectacular Iguazu Falls from both the Brazilian and Argentine sides.
- Take a thrilling boat ride beneath the falls for an amazing experience.

Day 10 - Departure:

- Depart from Foz do Iguaçu with memorable recollections of your adventure-filled vacation in Brazil.

Brazil offers a varied spectrum of unique interests, from family-friendly activities and LGBTQ+ travel to solitary excursions and adrenaline-pumping events. Embrace the warmth of Brazilian culture, immerse yourself in its gorgeous landscapes, and embark on fascinating experiences that appeal to your specific interests and hobbies. Whether you're traveling with family, exploring independently, or seeking exhilarating adventures, Brazil provides a limitless assortment of activities that will leave you with treasured memories and a better respect for this wonderful nation.

PRACTICAL TIPS FOR TRAVELERS

Currency and Money Matters

- **Currency:** The official currency of Brazil is the Brazilian Real (BRL). It's symbolized by the symbol "R$" and is usually referred to as "Real."

- **ATMs and Credit Cards:** ATMs are extensively accessible in cities and tourist locations. Major credit cards such as Visa and MasterCard are readily accepted in hotels, restaurants, and stores. However, it's always a good idea to bring some cash for smaller shops or in isolated regions.

- **Currency Exchange:** Exchange currency at banks or authorized exchange offices for the best rates.

Avoid exchanging money with unauthorized street sellers.

- **Tipping:** Tipping is not mandatory in Brazil, however, it's appreciated for excellent service. In restaurants, a service fee is frequently included in the bill, although an extra tip of roughly 10% is usual for good service.

Safety and Security

- **General Precautions:** Brazil, like any other nation, has its share of crime. Stay watchful and be careful in crowded locations, particularly in major cities. Avoid flaunting costly jewelry, electronics, or big quantities of cash.

- **Neighborhood Awareness:** Research and be educated on the safety of the communities you want to visit. Some places, particularly in big cities, may have higher crime rates.

- **Transportation Safety:** Use licensed taxis or ride-sharing services, particularly at night. Avoid unmarked cabs and consider utilizing trustworthy transportation apps.

- **Document Safety:** Keep critical papers like your passport, ID, and travel insurance in a safe and separate area, and take photocopies with you.

Local Etiquette and Customs

- **Greetings:** Brazilians are warm and sociable people. Greet with a grin, handshake, or cheek kiss (one on each side) for acquaintances.

- **Personal Space:** Brazilians are often outspoken and loving. Don't be startled if folks stand closer or touch during chats.

- **Language:** Portuguese is the official language, thus acquiring a few basic words might go a long way in relationships with locals.

- **Respect for Culture:** Respect local customs and traditions, particularly at holy places and indigenous communities. Seek permission before taking images of individuals or religious locations.

Internet and Connectivity

- **Wi-Fi and SIM Cards:** Many hotels, restaurants, and cafés provide free Wi-Fi, however, coverage may vary in more isolated regions. Consider acquiring a local SIM card for dependable data and calls throughout your stay.

- **Internet Cafes:** Internet cafes are less widespread anymore, although large cities still have several open for public use.

- **Mobile Applications:** Download essential mobile applications like Google Maps, Google Translate (for Portuguese), and transportation apps like Uber or local equivalents.

Language and Basic Phrases

The national language of Brazil is Portuguese, and although English is spoken in tourist areas, learning some basic Portuguese phrases can enrich your trip experience and make interactions with people more pleasurable. Here are some key Portuguese words to help you get started:

Greetings and Basic Expressions:
- Hello - Olá (oh-LAH)
- Good morning - Bom dia (BOHM DEE-ah)
- Good afternoon - Boa tarde (BOH-ah TAHR-deh)
- Good evening/Good night - Boa noite (BOH-ah NOH-eet)
- Thank you - Obrigado (for males) / Obrigada (for females) (oh-bree-GAH-doh/oh-bree-GAH-dah)
- You're welcome - De nada (dee NAH-dah)
- Yes - Sim (seem)
- No - Não (nah-oh)
- Excuse me/Pardon me - Com licença (kohm lee-SEN-sah)
- Sorry - Desculpe (deh-SKOO-pee)

Basic Conversation:

- How are you? - Como você está? (KOH-moh VOH-say es-TAH?)
- I'm fine, thank you - Estou bem, obrigado/a (es-TOH bayn, oh-bree-GAH-doh/oh-bree-GAH-dah)
- What is your name? - Qual é o seu nome? (KAHL eh oh say-oo NOH-mee?)
- My name is [your name] - Meu nome é [your name] (may-oo NOH-mee eh [your name])
- Please - Por favor (por fah-VOHR)

Directions and Travel:

- Where is...? - Onde fica...? (OHN-deh FEE-kah...?)
- How much is this? - Quanto custa isso? (KWAN-toh KOOS-tah EE-soh?)
- I don't understand - Eu não entendo (ay-oo NAH-oo ehn-TEN-doh)

- Can you help me? - Você pode me ajudar? (voh-SAY POH-deh may ah-zhoo-DAR?)
- I need a taxi - Eu preciso de um táxi (ay-oo preh-SEE-zoh dee oom TAH-ksee)

Food and Dining:

- Menu - Cardápio (kah-dah-PEE-oo)
- Water - Água (AH-gwah)
- Coffee - Café (kah-FEH)
- Beer - Cerveja (ser-VAY-zhah)
- Delicious - Delicioso/a (deh-lee-SYO-zoh/zah)
- Bill/Check - Conta (KON-tah)

Emergency Phrases:

- Help! - Socorro! (so-KOH-roh!)
- I need a doctor - Eu preciso de um médico (ay-oo preh-SEE-zoh dee oom MEH-dee-koo)
- Police - Polícia (poh-LEE-see-ah)

- I'm lost - Estou perdido/a (es-TOH PEHR-dee-doh/dah)

Traveling to Brazil is a rewarding experience. Stay informed about currency, prioritize safety, respect local customs, and adopt sustainable practices for a positive impact. Embrace the culture, landscapes, and hospitality responsibly. Learning basic Portuguese phrases shows respect and fosters warm interactions. Brazilians appreciate the effort, even with a few words. Enjoy your journey through Brazil responsibly and immerse yourself in its beauty and diversity.

SUSTAINABLE TRAVEL AND ECOTOURISM

Supporting Local Communities

Sustainable travel and ecotourism in Brazil go beyond merely admiring the natural beauty of the nation; they also include helping and strengthening local people. By participating in responsible tourism activities, tourists may positively influence the lives of local inhabitants and contribute to the preservation of their cultural heritage. Here are some ways to help local communities when vacationing in Brazil:

- **Choose Local Tour Operators:** Opt for local tour operators and guides who have a thorough awareness of the region and its communities. These operators typically return their gains to the local economy, helping small companies and community initiatives.

- **Buy Local Products:** Purchase souvenirs and handicrafts directly from local craftspeople and merchants. By purchasing original items, you support local lives and help preserve traditional workmanship.

- **Dine at Local Eateries:** Instead of patronizing multinational chain restaurants, go for locally-owned eateries and street sellers. Not only will you experience traditional Brazilian cuisine, but you'll also support the local food sector.

- **Respect Local Culture:** Embrace and respect the customs and traditions of the communities you visit. Learn about local etiquette, clothing rules, and procedures to prevent accidental offending.

- **Volunteer Responsibly:** If you choose to volunteer on your trip, investigate the organizations extensively to verify they have a beneficial influence on the community. Volunteering options that concentrate on education, conservation, and community development may be gratifying and useful.

Reducing Environmental Impact

As a responsible traveler, it's crucial to limit your environmental imprint during your vacation to Brazil. The country's unique ecosystems are sensitive and require preservation from unsustainable activities. Here are some techniques to lessen your environmental impact:

- **Use Reusable Water Bottles:** Carry a reusable water bottle and refill it at filtered water stations to decrease plastic waste.

- **Avoid Single-Use Plastics:** Say goodbye to single-use plastics such as straws, bags, and cutlery. Bring reusable alternatives like cloth bags and metal straws.

- **Conserve Water and Energy:** Practice water and energy saving in lodgings by reusing towels, and turning off lights, and air conditioning when not required.

- **Responsible Waste Disposal:** Dispose of waste correctly, using designated recycling containers wherever feasible. Avoid trash and participate in scheduled beach or environmental cleanups.

- **Choose Sustainable Transit:** Use public transit, walk, or bike wherever practicable. If driving is unavoidable, carpool with other tourists or consider renting an electric or hybrid vehicle.

- **Support Sustainable Initiatives:** Patronize institutions and activities that highlight sustainable practices and conservation initiatives.

Eco-friendly Accommodation

Eco-friendly lodgings in Brazil promote sustainable techniques and reduce their environmental effect. These businesses frequently undertake measures such as energy efficiency, water conservation, waste reduction, and assistance for local communities. When selecting eco-friendly housing, seek the following features:

- **Energy Conservation:** Eco-friendly lodgings utilize energy-efficient equipment, lights, and heating/cooling systems to decrease energy use.

- **Water Management:** These institutions adopt water-saving methods, such as low-flow toilets and showers, rainwater harvesting, and water recycling.

- **Sustainable Materials:** Look for lodgings that employ sustainable construction materials, furnishings, and designs that have a low environmental effect.

- **Local Sourcing:** Eco-friendly enterprises frequently favor locally-sourced items and ingredients to support the local economy and decrease carbon emissions from transportation.

- **Community Engagement:** Accommodations that are devoted to sustainability typically interact with local communities and promote social activities.

- **Certificates:** Look for certificates such as LEED (Leadership in Energy and Environmental Design) or sustainable tourism certifications that certify the accommodation's eco-friendly operations.

Respectful Interactions with Wildlife

Brazil is home to some of the world's most varied and unusual species, and as tourists, it's vital to view animals responsibly to maintain their natural habitats and habits. Here are some rules for polite encounters with wildlife:

- **Observe from a Distance:** When meeting wild creatures, keep a safe and respectful distance. Use binoculars or a zoom lens for a closer look without creating disruption.

- **No Feeding:** Never feed wild animals, since it might disturb their normal diet and behavior, and can lead to health concerns.

- **Avoid Touching:** Refrain from touching, stroking, or trying to engage physically with wild animals. This may be distressing for them and may also pose hazards to your safety.

- **Stay Quiet and Calm:** Loud sounds and quick movements might alarm animals. Observe softly and calmly to prevent disturbing the animals.

- **Do Not Chase or Corner:** Avoid pursuing or cornering animals. Give them room and freedom to move and act normally.

- **Respect Protected Areas:** Follow established pathways and standards in national parks and protected areas. These restrictions are in place to safeguard animals and their habitats.

- **No Flash Photography:** Flash photography may shock and disorient animals, particularly nocturnal species. Avoid using flash while photographing animals.

- **Avoid Wildlife Selfies:** Refrain from taking selfies with animals, since it might lead to hazardous circumstances and invasive encounters.

- **Marine Wildlife:** When indulging in aquatic sports, such as snorkeling or diving, avoid harming or disturbing marine life, particularly corals and sea critters.

By practicing sustainable travel and respecting animals, tourists can play an important part in safeguarding Brazil's natural riches and ensuring that future generations may enjoy the country's extraordinary biodiversity. Responsible tourism develops a peaceful interaction between tourists and the environment, and it enables visitors to enjoy the beauty of Brazil while having a good influence on its ecosystems and local people.

Printed in Great Britain
by Amazon